-Never Stop Pursuing Your Dreams

SUCCESS UNDER CONSTRUCTION

Kenneth Page

SUCCESS UNDER CONSTRUCTION

A GUIDE FOR MATURING PEOPLE

31 DAY DEVOTIONAL

KENNETH PAGE

ISBN-13: 978-0692551868 (KennethPage)

ISBN-10: 0692551867

I would like to dedicate this first book to my mother Rose,

Who would never accept mediocrity,

And always pushed me to do better.

Thank You

Proverbs 29:18 (KJV)
*Where there is no vision, the people perish: but
he that keepeth the law, happy is he.*

GOAL SETTING

the process of deciding what you want to
accomplish and then preparing a plan to achieve
the results that you want

Goal setting has two major components;
(1) Setting the goal and (2) making a plan to
achieve the goal. If you don't have a goal set,
what direction will you be going or if you only
have a goal and don't have a plan to achieve it,
then how will you accomplish It.?

When Nehemiah heard that the great
wall around his hometown, Jerusalem, had been
torn down, he became very sad. So he set a
goal to rebuild the wall and made a plan to do
so. Because other people did not support him or
believe in what he was doing, they tried to
distract him and sabotage the work he was
trying to accomplish. But because Nehemiah
had set a goal, he was able to avoid being
distracted, make the right decisions, and
accomplish what he set out to do despite all the
distractions and negative influences around him.

If we want to be the best person that we
can be and become successful in our lives, then
we have to set GOOD goals and make a plan to
achieve them. When we do not have a goal,
something to aim for and a plan to achieve it, we
can become distracted and start to make bad
decisions. Bad decisions have bad
consequences and these will not help us

become the best person that we can be and it will not help us become successful. Not only does setting a goal help us achieve something, it also helps keep us from making the wrong decisions.

We need to set goals in our lives if we want to be successful. Setting a goal and taking the proper steps to complete the goal will help keep us focused, achieve something, and stay out of trouble. Think of what you want to accomplish within sports or in the classroom or with your behavior; make a plan on how to do it, then do it. Challenge yourself to set goals in your life, small and big, and accomplish them.

Scripture to Remember

Habakkuk 2:2 Write the vision; make it plain on tablets, so he may run who reads it (ESV)

Questions for Growth

1. Why is important to have goals in your life?
2. What is 1 short term and 1 long term goal that you have? If you do not have one, create one. (short term is less than a year)
3. What do you have to do to accomplish these two goals?

1 Samuel 16:7 (ESV)
*But the Lord said to Samuel, "Do not look on his
appearance or on the height of his stature,
because I have rejected him. For the Lord sees
not as man sees: man looks on the outward
appearance, but the Lord looks on the heart."*

CHARACTER

the way someone thinks, feels, and behaves;
someone's personality

The character of a person is shown by
what they will do when nobody else is looking.
It's easier to do the right thing when someone is
there to hold you accountable, but character
asks this question; do you do the right thing
when nobody is looking?

God refers to David as "a man after my
own heart" and he is the only person in the bible
described like this. Samuel was sent out to find
the next king of Israel and was sent to the house
of Jesse. Jesse had about eight sons and David
was his youngest and smallest son. Samuel
thought God would select the biggest and
strongest looking son, but God wanted the one
with the most character.

Character is what defines you. It is what
people see in you based off what you show
through your words and actions. Your character
will determine the quality of people that want to
be around you and what people would be willing
to do or sacrifice for you. A person with good

character usually is a happier person, gets in trouble less, and becomes more successful than people with bad character.

Overall, your character describes the type of person that you are. People determine your character based off what they see you do. Think about how you act when no one else is watching. If someone were to see you in times like this, would they be able to say you are a good person or a bad person? Challenge yourself to behave like you have good character when people are looking and more importantly, when people are not looking.

Scripture to Remember

Galatians 5:22-23 But the fruit of the Spirit is love, joy, peace, patience, kindness, goodness, faithfulness, gentleness, self-control; against such things there is no law. (WEB)

Questions for Growth

1. Which fruit of the spirit are you best at and how do you know?
2. Which fruit of the spirit are you most lacking in and how do you know?
3. What can you start doing to improve the quality you listed in #2

Proverbs 13: 20 (ESV)
*Whoever walks with the wise becomes wise,
but the companion of fools will suffer harm*

INFLUENCE

the power to effect a person's character,
development, behavior, and opinions without
force

Influence is when you change someone in an indirect way. Seeing a kid hug their parents may influence you to call your parents. Or seeing a lot of your family in the military may influence you to join the military. Influence is simply to play a part in the choices that someone else makes whether you mean to or not.

When the Bible talks about the flesh and the spirit, it is talking about influences. Influence is very important and can steer someone in the right or wrong direction. God gives much wisdom on the people that you surround yourself with. The Bible tells us that if we want to make better decisions, then we should surround ourselves with good influences.

Influence is a key component in our lives. It plays a larger role than what we think it actually does. You will become whatever influences you the most. Therefore, if we want to make better decisions and have a successful life, then we must also surround ourselves with people who would influence us to make better decisions and have a successful life.

Influence is the ability to produce an effect upon others. The way a person influences us is often times done indirectly however, what we see and hear is what influences us the most. It is important that we position ourselves to see and hear the right things so that we can have good influences in our lives. Think about the people you surround yourself with. How do they influence you or what have you changed about yourself that is similar to them? Challenge yourself to pay attention to influences and surround yourself with good ones.

Scripture to Remember

1 Corinthians 15:33 Do not be misled: "Bad company corrupts good character. (NIV)

Questions for Growth

1. Do your words and behavior influence people to become better?
2. How can you control what influences you the most?
3. Who are people in your life that are good influences?

Philippians 2:14 (ESV)
Do all things without grumbling or disputing

ATTITUDE

the way you think and feel about someone or
something

Attitude often refers to what is going on
inside a person's head but more times than not,
your attitude is shown by your behaviors and
your actions. When we talk about what attitude a
person has, we are looking at how they are
acting, talking, or looking. We then think about
what they must be feeling to act, talk, or look the
way that they do.

When people grumble (complain) and
dispute (fight) all the time, we generally think of
this person as having a bad attitude. They don't
have a bad attitude because they are grumbling
and disputing; they are grumbling and disputing
because they have a bad attitude. We are
supposed to maintain a good attitude regardless
of what we are doing.

It is often said that your attitude
determines your altitude. This is very true
because your behavior is a reflection of your
attitude and your attitude determines what type
of behavior you will have. When people behave
in a negative way (saying and doing hurtful,
mean, or wrong things), other people don't want
to be around them which is the same as saying
when people have bad attitudes, no one wants

to be around them. If you have a good positive attitude, you will have better behavior, more people will want to be around you, and more opportunities will be available for you.

With our attitudes playing a major role in the type of behavior that we have, it is very important that we are conscience about this and strive to maintain a good positive attitude. This does not mean that we have to feel good at all times, but it does mean that we can think in a more positive way. Has someone ever told you that your attitude needs improvement or that you have a nasty attitude? Challenge yourself to have a more positive attitude about your life, situation, and circumstances.

Scripture to Remember

Proverbs 17:22 A joyful heart is good medicine, But a broken spirit dries up the bones. (ESV)

Questions for Growth

1. How has your attitude affected your life?
2. Why or why not is it important for you to have a good attitude?
3. What is something you can do to help improve your attitude?

1 Timothy 4:12 (NIV)
*Don't let anyone look down on you because you
are young, but set an example for the believers
in speech, in conduct, in love, in faith and in
purity.*

ROLE -MODEL

a person who serves as a model that someone
should imitate

A role-model is someone that you want
to be like. For us, we should use role-models in
two ways for our lives. (1) We should have a
good role-model or someone that we should
imitate. (2) We should serve to be a good role-
model to others or behave in a way that would
be good if others imitated us.

Many characters in the Bible serve as a
great role-model. David serves as a great role-
model for honesty in communicating with God as
we read his prayers in Psalms. Noah's building
of the Ark in good weather is a great role-model
for obedience and belief in God's word. Job is a
great role-model for trusting God in hard times.
But there is no greater role-model than Jesus
the Christ. When we call ourselves Christians,
what we are saying is that we want to be like
Christ. A Christian is to let Jesus be their role-
model and aim to do things the way He did
them.

Role-models are important because
they help direct your life. If you do what

someone does, you will get what they got. If you do what a successful person does, that will steer you towards success. If you do what a bum does, that will steer you towards being a bum. If you aim to make yourself a model to the generation before you, it will help keep you on the right path.

Role-models are people that we want to be like. It is very important that we have a good role model in our lives to help guide our actions while also being a role model to others to help sustain our good actions. Think about the people around you. Do you serve as a good role model to them? Challenge yourself to find a role model that you can imitate while being a role model to others.

Scripture to Remember

Titus 2:7 in all things show yourself to be an example of good deeds... (NASB)

Questions for Growth

1. Who are you being a good role-model to?
2. How can good role-models influence your life?
3. Who are some of your role-models and why?

Proverbs 12:22 (ESV)
*Lying lips are an abomination to the Lord, but
those who act faithfully are his delight.*

HONESTY

good and truthful, not hiding the truth about
someone or something

Honesty talks about a person who is
honest or tells the truth. They are honorable in
their principles, intentions, and actions. Honest
people are fair people. Honesty people are
trustworthy people.

God hates a lying tongue; he despises
anyone who does not tell the truth. There once
was a man and a woman names Ananias and
Sapphira who worked with the church. They
were not honest about what they were doing
with the money. When they got caught, instead
of telling the truth, they continued to lie. Because
of their lies and stealing and false ways, they
were immediately judged and died right their on
the spot.

We have to be able to tell the truth at all
times. We have to be honest people. If you
make a habit of lying, people will not believe you
and when you really need some help or you are
actually telling the truth for once, no one will
believe you because you lied to them before.
Your level of honesty will determine how people
interact with you and how much people trust
you.

Being honest means that you are telling the truth. It affects my trustworthiness or how much people can trust me. Where there are lies, there is no trust. Think about how much you communicate with people. Do you find yourself being honest in all situations, even the really tough ones, or do you find yourself telling lies? Challenge yourself to always be honest, no matter what the circumstances are.

Scripture to Remember

John 8:32 And you will know the truth, and the truth will set you free. (ESV)

Questions for Growth

1. What does "the truth will set you free" mean to you?
2. What makes it hard for you to be honest sometimes?
3. Is honesty always important? Why or why not?

Deuteronomy 30: 19 (ESV)
*I call heaven and earth to witness against you
today, that I have set before you life and death,
blessing and curse. Therefore choose life, that
you and your offspring may live.*

DECISION MAKING

the action or process of making decisions,
especially important ones.

Decision Making is when we have to
make a choice to do or not do something. These
decisions can be as small as what shirt you will
wear to something as big as where you will go to
school or as important as how you will respond
to things.

When we are making decisions, we
should always make the choice that gives the
most honor back to God. God says that we have
free will, the ability to make our own decisions,
and that we will always have the opportunity to
either do the right thing or the wrong thing. This
means that most of the time, we will have to
make a decision to either do right or do wrong.
When we choose to do the right thing, we are
making wise decisions which ultimately will
benefit ourselves and our lives.

It is impossible to go a long time without
being faced with a decision to make. It is
important that more times than not, we make the
right decisions. As we continuously make the
right decisions, we will see good things happen
in our lives. If we make wrong decisions, we will
see bad things happen in our lives. To get the
most out of life and be the best person that you

can be, you need to have the ability to make good decisions. If we spend time praying, listening to our parents and older people, and studying the Word of God, we will be able to make the right decisions which ultimately will lead to a happier life.

We have to be able to make the right decision. We are forever faced with choices and it is how we handle these choices that shape our lives; for our lives are just a sum total of all the choices that we make. Think about the situations that you find yourself in and the choices that you choose to make; do you see how they are related to one another? Challenge yourself to make the right decisions in everything that you do and when you don't know what the right thing to do is, challenge yourself to get advice from a person who makes good decisions on a regular basis.

Scripture to Remember

Proverbs 3:5 Trust in the Lord with all your heart, and do not lean on your own understanding. (NIV)

Questions for Growth

1. How can studying the Bible help you improve your decision making skills?
2. How can the people you spend your time with effect the decisions that you make?
3. Who is someone that you can go to for good advice?

Proverbs 21:3 (NIV)
*To do what is right and just is more acceptable
to the LORD than sacrifice.*

INTEGRITY

the quality of being honest

Integrity talks about how honest a person is. Integrity also talks about if a person has good morals or if they follow ethical principles. You could find yourself in a situation where you have the power or authority to do something, but it may not be appropriate to do. You can trust that a person of good integrity would make the right decision in situations like these.

All throughout scripture, we can see where God required sacrifices to be made to him. No doubt about it, sacrifices were very important; but here we see that He would rather a person do the right thing than to make sacrifices. God commands us to love one another and one aspect of that is in how we treat people. To God, he would be more pleased with the person who does the right thing and behaves with good moral principles than the person who treats people unfairly but follows His other rules.

When people think of you, you want them to think of you as having good integrity. A person of good integrity is viewed as trustworthy and just an all-around good person. It is hard to be considered for promotions or opportunities in life if people don't think of you as having good integrity. Your level of integrity is directly correlated to the way that people perceive you. Their perspective of you can either open doors for your life or close them.

A person with integrity is a person who is honest and uses sound judgment. Think about the type of people that you would prefer to spend your time with and the type of people you don't mind helping. Would you prefer the person with or without integrity? Challenge yourself to be honest with yourself and with other people while also following ethical and moral principles.

Scripture to Remember

Proverbs 28:6 Better is a poor man who walks in his integrity than a rich man who is crooked in his ways. (ESV)

Questions for Growth

1. Do you agree with the observation from Proverbs 28:6? Why or Why not?
2. How do ethical and moral principles affect society?
3. How can having more integrity affect your life?

Galatians 6:7 (ESV)
*Do not be deceived: God is not mocked, for
whatever one sows, that will he also reap.*

CONSEQUENCES

the result or outcome of an event; what happens
next

All actions have consequences.
Consequences are what happen next based on
what we do now. It is a sequence of events
where what happens next is directly related to
what happens now.

In the long run, consequences match
the action; if I have good actions, I'll have good
consequences and if I have bad actions I will
have bad consequences. Sometimes people do
bad things and think that something good will
happen to them because of it. God says that
whatever a person sows, that is what they will
reap. This means that whatever you do will be
done back to you.

There will always be consequences to
our actions. We will always be doing something
in life so there will always be some kind of
consequence. Some consequences are
immediate and some are long term but no
matter how you look at it, all actions will have a
consequence. It is important that we remember
the consequences of our actions; if I want to
have a good life, then I need to have good
actions so that the consequences of my actions

are also good. If you hate being punished, don't do things that cause you to get punished. This is exactly what all actions have consequences mean, if you can't do the time, don't do the crime.

We must always remember that what you do today affects what you will have tomorrow. So it is important that we understand all actions have consequences. We can control the action, not the consequence. Have you ever found yourself in a situation that you didn't like being in? What actions did you take to wind up with the consequences that you were in? Challenge yourself to think about the consequences of your actions before you do them. Aim to base your actions off the consequences you would like to see.

Scripture to Remember

Luke 6:38 Give, and it will be given to you, Good measure, pressed down, shaken together, running over, will be put into your lap. For with the measure you use it will be measured back to you. (ESV)

Questions for Growth

1. What does Luke 6:38 mean to you?
2. Why is it important to think about the consequences of your actions?
3. How can considering the consequences of your actions help make your life better?

Luke 12:48 (ESV)
...Everyone to whom much was given, of him much will be required, and from him to whom they entrusted much, they will demand the more

RESPONSIBILITY

having a duty to deal with something or having control over someone else's well being

Responsibility means to be responsible. It means that you have an obligation or requirement to take care of a situation or a person, and you do it. A responsible person can be depended on and a responsible person can be trusted. They will do what is right or what is expected of them to do.

Whenever God would assign anybody a task, what he was giving them was responsibility for a thing or a group of people. There was an expectancy that whatever responsibility was given to that person would be handled properly and with care. When God created man, he gave us dominion, or power, over all the earth and the animals on the earth. He made us responsible for the well-being of the animals and the earth. Every person that God ever created was given some type of responsibility, whether it was big or small.

We have to be responsible for whatever we have to take care of. When kids are young, their parents have to take responsibility for them. Responsible parents would do what needs to be done so that the children are taken care of. We all have been given a life and we have to take responsibility for it. If we want to be successful at anything, we have to be responsible enough to do the right thing and what is expected or needed in order to achieve it.

Being responsible means that you are doing the right thing and doing what is needed so that the person or thing you are responsible for has a good outcome. When we neglect our responsibilities, we allow things to pile up on top of us. Think about anything that you are supposed to be taking care of. Are you being responsible with it? Challenge yourself to do the right thing and take care of anything that you are supposed to take care of.

Scripture to Remember

Galatians 6:5 for each one is to carry their own load (NIV)

Questions for Growth

1. What are some of the things that you are responsible for? Are you being responsible?
2. How does neglecting responsibilities affect you?
3. Why is it important to be a responsible person?

Titus 2: 11-12 (NASB)
*For the grace of God has appeared, bringing
salvation to all men, instructing us to deny
ungodliness and worldly desires and to live
sensibly, righteously and godly in the present
age*

SELF – CONTROL

the ability to control oneself, in particular one's
emotions and desires or the expression of them
in one's behavior, especially in difficult
situations.

Self - control means exactly what it
says, control over yourself. If you get mad and
do something out of anger, anger is in control of
you, not you. Self - control is the ability to make
the right decisions no matter what the situation
is and what is going on around you.

The Bible tells us on multiple occasions
that there are things that we should and should
not do. When Adam and Eve ate the fruit of the
tree that God told them not to, they were not
using allot of self-control. They knew what the
right thing to do was, but they could not control
themselves enough to do the right thing. If Adam
and Eve used more self-control, they would not
have gotten into the trouble that they got into.

If we have good self-control, we will
always choose the right thing to do no matter
how we are feeling. And when we choose the
right thing to do, make good decisions, we often

have a good outcome. Without self-control, that could lead us into doing many things that we know we should not be doing, bad decision making. And these bad decisions have consequences that will be bad as well. If we want to make good decisions and accomplish anything in life, we are going to have to have self-control.

Self-control is just another term for having discipline. If we have the ability to control ourselves, we can accomplish anything that we set out to do and become successful. What do you think about your ability to control yourself and do the right thing no matter what? Challenge yourself to stay in control of your emotions and actions and to make the right decisions no matter what is going on around you or what is happening to you.

Scripture to Remember

Proverbs 25:28 A man without self-control is like a city broken into and left without walls. (ESV)

Questions for Growth

1. How can a lack of self-control be dangerous?
2. Why is it not a good idea to follow your emotions all the time?
3. What is something you can do to help improve your level of self-control?

Romans 14:12 (ESV)
So then each of us will give an account of himself to God.

ACCOUNTABILITY

an obligation or willingness to accept responsibility or to account for one's actions

Being accountable not only means being responsible for something, but also means being answerable for your actions. Accountability is something you hold a person to only after a task is done or not done. If a person is held accountable for something, they are required to explain their actions or decisions to someone else.

God has given all of us free will meaning that we can make any choice that we want to make. But we will also have to answer for all of these things. One day we will have to give an account for all the good and bad things that we did in our lives. When God would send someone on a mission to complete them, they would always have to give an explanation to God about what they did and why they did it. God always holds us accountable for our words and actions because we have to be responsible for our own words and actions.

Accountability helps a person be more responsible for their actions. If I never have to answer for what I do, then I don't have a good reason to do the right thing. If I am unable to be held accountable for something, then I don't deserve to have that responsibility and I also don't deserve to have those benefits either. If I can be held accountable for something, it means that I am going to be responsible for what was given to me and I'm going to do my very best with it.

Accountability is the other side of responsibility that says, you can trust me to take care of my responsibilities and if I don't, it is my fault that it is not completed and I will take the consequences that come from not being responsible. Think about some of the things that you are responsible for. Are people able to hold you accountable for those things and your actions? Challenge yourself to want to be held accountable for the things you are supposed to do and the things that you said you would do.

Scripture to Remember

Hebrews 4:13 And no creature is hidden from his sight, but all are naked and exposed to the eyes of him to whom we must give account. (ESV)

Questions for Growth

1. What does accountability mean to you?
2. What is one thing that you should start being held accountable for, big or small?
3. Who can you find to hold you accountable for this?

Exodus 16:4 (NIV)
Then the Lord said to Moses, "I will rain down bread from heaven for you. The people are to go out each day and gather enough for that day. In this way I will test them and see whether they will follow my instructions

DISCIPLINE

self-controlled; mastered from within

To be disciplined means that you do what is necessary, even if you don't like doing it or don't feel like doing it. A person who wants to have a healthy body will have to be disciplined in their eating habits. Through discipline, they would choose fruits instead of desserts even though they would rather have a piece of cake instead of an apple. To have discipline is to have the ability to do what is right and what is necessary despite how you may be feeling.

When the Lord wanted to see how disciplined the people of Israel were, he gave them a test. They were wandering through the wilderness and got hungry and asked for food. So each day, God would make bread rain down from the sky, more than they needed, but they were only supposed to take what they needed and leave the rest. If they were being discipline, they would have done the right thing and followed His instructions by only taking what they needed.

If we are setting goals in our life and trying to accomplish them, we will have to be disciplined. If we want to be successful in life we have to be disciplined. Discipline helps you make the right choices and forces you to only do things that are good for you and your life. Discipline means going to bed on time, not being late to places, completing assignments on time, not being greedy, following rules, and everything else like that. We have to have discipline to stay on the right track and accomplish our goals in life.

Discipline is about doing the right thing or doing what is necessary all the time; when you feel like it and when you don't, or when you like doing it and when you hate doing it. Think about any goals you have set or any tasks that you have to do. Are you disciplined enough to complete them? Challenge yourself to have the discipline that you need in the area that you need it.

Scripture to Remember

Titus 1:8 Rather, he must be hospitable, one who loves what is good, who is self-controlled, upright, holy and disciplined. (NIV)

Questions for Growth

1. Why is discipline important in our lives?
2. What is something that you can do to be more disciplined?
3. How does punishment for doing the wrong thing increase your level of discipline?

Colossians 3:23 (ESV)
*Whatever you do, work heartily, as for the Lord
and not for men*

WORK ETHIC

a belief in the benefits and importance of hard
work

When we talk about work ethic, we are talking about the way a person works and normally in a good way. A person who has a good work ethic is going to be someone who works hard at any and everything that they do.

The Bible is full of characters and examples of people who worked hard. Every person that God ever called to do anything for him had to have a great work ethic. Noah built the ark; David fought off armies; and prophets traveled across countries to deliver messages. While everybody that God ever used was very unique and different from one another, they all had one thing in common, they knew how to work.

Whether you are dealing with class, sports, arts, or games; you have to have a great work ethic to be successful at it. Nothing in life worth having is easy and it's going to take work, hard work, to be successful or great. People without a good work ethic, lazy people, will have a hard life and will not be successful in their lives. Lazy people become broke and poor people.

Work ethic describes a person's willingness to do everything it takes to get the job done. A person's work ethic describes how they approach every situation, not just one area. Think about the different things that you currently have to do in your days. Can you say that you have a good work ethic based on all of those? Challenge yourself to develop your work ethic by working hard in everything that you do.

Scripture to Remember

Proverbs 10:4 Lazy hands make for poverty, but diligent hands bring wealth (NIV)

Questions for Growth

1. How can laziness lead to being poor?
2. Why is it important to have a good and strong work ethic?
3. What are somethings you can do to improve your work ethic?

Genesis 2:18 (NIV)
...It is not good that the man should be alone...

RELATIONAL

to be in relation with someone or something
else; the way in which two or more people or
things relate to one another

To be relational means that you can
maintain a relationship with another person.
Relational always refers to the way in which you
relate with another person.

In the beginning when God created the
first man Adam, He made it clear that it was not
good for man to be alone. From that time on, we
can see that nothing that man accomplished
was done alone. Moses needed help from Aaron
when he was freeing the Israelites. David
needed help from Johnathon to learn the rules of
the kingdom. Jesus needed help from the
disciples to spread His ministry. All throughout
the Bible are examples of men accomplishing
things but they did it with the help of others.
They had to have a relationship with another
person to complete their task.

In life, it is important to have
relationships with other people. No one person
knows everything and no one person can do
everything. However, accomplishing certain
tasks or goals requires multiple skills, abilities,
and knowledge. Therefore, we must be able to
reach out to other people who can do things that

we may not be able to do on our own. This need for other people requires us to be able to maintain a relationship with someone else. It is also good to have people you can talk to. Many times, it is just good to have a friend to talk to about certain things. This also requires us to be relational people because holding stuff in creates stress and makes it hard to focus, which can hinder your success.

A relational person is a person who can maintain a relationship with someone else. We need relationships to help us out when we need it and we need relationships for friendships. Think about the interactions that you have with people. Are you a relational person? Challenge yourself to build and maintain relationships with multiple people and be open to the differences that others may have.

Scripture to Remember

Proverbs 15: 22 Without counsel plans fail, but with many advisers they succeed. (ESV)

Questions for Growth

1. How can having an advisor, mentor, or confidant be beneficial to your life?
2. Why do you need relationships in your life?
3. What can you do to maintain the relationships that you currently have?

Daniel 6:3 (KJV)
Then this Daniel was preferred above the presidents and princes, because an excellent spirit was in him; and the king thought to set him over the whole realm.

EXCELLENCE

the quality of being outstanding or extremely good

Excellence is striving to be the very best in whatever it is you are doing. Excellence is beyond great, its being exceptional, phenomenal... excellent!

Daniel was a prophet for God and became a great political figure in his time as well. What's amazing about Daniel is that he started out as a slave. But the way he conducted himself with excellence lead the king to greatly promote him. Even though he did not start out in the best situation, his excellence moved him higher and farther in life than he could've imagined.

Excellence is something that you have carry over your life. It's a way of life that you have to live. Being excellent takes hard work but it can be done if you are determined and the benefits from excellence are great. Excellence in your life could be the key that takes you over the top of success.

Striving for excellence means that I am trying to be the very best that I can be and do the very best job that I can possibly do. Your life can only be benefitted by striving for excellence. Think about the things you want in life and the things you currently do in life. Are you striving to be the very best that you can be and doing the best job that you can do? Challenge yourself to always strive for excellence in everything that you do.

Scripture to Remember

Philippians 4:8 Finally, brothers, whatever is true, whatever is honorable, whatever is just, whatever is pure, whatever is lovely, whatever is commendable, if there is any excellence, if there is anything worthy of praise, think about these things. (ESV)

Questions for Growth

1. What does excellence mean to you?
2. Why is important to strive to be excellent?
3. What is something currently in your life that you can become excellent in and how will you do it?

John 3:16 (KJV)
For God so loved the world, that he gave his only begotten Son, that whosoever believeth in him should not perish, but have everlasting life.

SACRIFICE

the act of giving up one thing in order to receive something more valuable

A sacrifice is when you give up one thing in order to receive something better. Usually the thing that you are sacrificing is something that you want or sometimes may even need. However, the thing that you are giving up is necessary in order to receive that reward. If you want a reward (or to receive something better), you have to make a sacrifice (or give up something that you like).

When God wanted to give us the reward of eternal life, a sacrifice had to be made. He sacrificed his only begotten son so that we could have the reward of eternal life. We received the reward, but a sacrifice had to first be made. God gave up something that He loved so that someone else, us, could receive the reward.

We have to make sacrifices in order to get things that we or someone else may want or need. When a child needs clothes, a parent has to sacrifice some money. If a student wants to get an A on their next exam, they would have to sacrifice their time to study. If you want to be successful, you'll have to sacrifice some things in your life in order to get it. If you are never willing to give up something, you will never get something else.

Sacrifice is giving up something in order to receive something better. If sacrifices aren't made, nothing will be achieved. Think about some of the things that you want that you don't have yet. Are you making the necessary sacrifices in order to get it? Challenge yourself to let go of whatever is needed in order to achieve your goal.

Scripture to Remember

Hebrews 13:16 And do not forget to do good and to share with others, for with such sacrifices God is pleased. (NIV)

Questions for Growth

1. How does making sacrifices for other people affect the community?
2. How would your life be if no one made sacrifices for you?
3. What is something that you can sacrifice to improve your life?

James 1:12 (NIV)
Blessed is the one who perseveres under trial
because, having stood the test, that person will
receive the crown of life that the Lord has
promised to those who love him.

PERSEVERANCE

steady persistence in a course of action, a
purpose, a state, etc., especially in spite of
difficulties, obstacles, or discouragement.

Perseverance is not giving up. It is the
striving to accomplish something and finishing it
regardless of how hard it becomes to do it.
Perseverance is seeing something through all
the way to the end.

Many times, situations do not go the
way that they are planned. When Jacob fell in
love with Rachel, he wanted to do anything to be
with her. He agreed to work seven years to
receive her as his wife but was tricked. Jacob
then had to work 14 years before he was able to
have the woman he loved as his wife. What
Jacob had to do was persevere through those
last seven years. He could have quit and
decided to not do everything he needed to do to
have Rachel as his wife, but he didn't. When
times got hard and it seemed better to give up
on his goal, he didn't and worked even harder.

As we go on with our lives, it seems like
something always comes up to get in the way. It
seems like something that was supposed to be
easy to do somehow doesn't seem so easy once
we start or something will come up to make the
job harder to finish. It is times like this when we

must persevere. Nothing in life worth having is easy to get so if we want good things in our lives, we are going to have to persevere through the hard times.

Ultimately, when we want to achieve something, we have to be willing to do everything that it takes to achieve what we wanted even if that means working through the hard times. Do you find yourself wanting to quit something when it gets too hard? Whenever you have a goal set to do something, think of every way you can accomplish the goal instead of looking for excuses to stop. Challenge yourself to make ways, not excuses.

Scripture to Remember

Galatians 6:9 Let us not become weary in doing good, for at the proper time we will reap a harvest if we do not give up. (NIV)

Questions for Growth

1. What does perseverance mean to you?
2. Why does perseverance lead to success?
3. What is something that you need to persevere at and how will you do it?

Philippians 2:3 (ESV)
*Do nothing from selfish ambition or conceit, but
in humility count others as more significant than
yourselves.*

HUMILITY

not proud: not thinking of yourself as better than
other people

Being humble means that you are not
arrogant, prideful, or spend allot of time
bragging. A humble person is someone who no
matter what they have accomplished in their life,
never thinks that they are better than other
people.

The Bible points out that we should not
always be concerned with our own interests; that
we should do something to benefit other people.
If we are to be like Christ, then we should imitate
his humility, who, though he was in the form of
God, did not count equality with God a thing to
be grasped, but emptied himself, by taking the
form of a servant, being born in the likeness of
men. And being found in human form, he
humbled himself by becoming obedient to the
point of death, even death on a cross. The
greatest act of humility was when Jesus went to
the cross to save us.

Humble people often take the time to
help other people because they are concerned
with the interest of other people as well. The
opposite of being humble is having too much

pride. Often times, pride comes right before
something bad is about to happen. If we keep
ourselves humble, we not only make ourselves a
better person and help out the people around
us, but we help put ourselves into a position
where we can receive good things. So being
humble helps out you and another person while
being prideful doesn't help anybody.

Humility is a characteristic that we all
need to have. It is good when we take the time
to help other people out because we don't think
that we are better than they are. No one likes a
prideful, arrogant, and selfish person and no one
wants to be around them either. Think about
how you treat people. Are you the type of person
to only think about yourself, or do you take the
time to help other people out? Challenge
yourself to not think arrogantly of yourself while
trying to help out as many people as you can.

Scripture to Remember

Proverbs 18:12 Before a downfall the heart is
haughty, but humility comes before honor. (NIV)

Questions for Growth

1. What does humility mean to you?
2. How do you feel after you interact with a
   humble person?
3. How could the community benefit if
   more people were humble?

1 Corinthians 9: 24 (ESV)
*Do you not know that in a race all the runners
run, but only one receives the prize? So run that
you may obtain it.*

DETERMINATION

the quality of never giving up

Determination is simply never giving up.
A determined person does not let go of whatever
they are determined to accomplish. They do
whatever has to be done to finish the job. It
takes determination to get through the hard
times when you are ready to quit.

Often times in the Bible, people were
assigned tasks to do or complete. Somewhere
along the line, they ran into some opposition or
something that would make it hard for them to
complete their task. When Moses was sent to
free the people of Israel, he had to go plead to
the Pharaoh ten different times before the
Pharaoh would let them go. After the Pharaoh
let the people go, he sent armies to chase them
down. But still, Moses was so determined to free
the people that he led them through the Red
Sea to safety. Moses had a mission and came
against much opposition, but his determination
to finish the job helped him complete it.

We all have something that we want to
do in our lives. If we have any goal set for
ourselves, it is going to take determination to
complete it. Life is hard and completing things in

life is just as hard. For whatever we want, we have to be determined to finish it if we really want to complete that task. When times get hard and we are ready to quit, we have to be determined to keep going anyway. When things get difficult and we want to throw the towel in, we have to be determined to not give up.

Determination is simply doing whatever I have to do to finish the job. It is a commitment to get the job done when times are hard. It is not making excuses but only looking for a solution to do. Think about something that you were supposed to do and what happened when it got hard. Are you the type of person to quit when times get tough or are you the type to find a way to get it done? Challenge yourself to not make excuses to quit when times get hard in anything that you do.

Scripture to Remember

2 Timothy 4:7 I have fought the good fight, I have finished the race, I have kept the faith (NIV)

Questions for Growth

1. What would it feel like to recite 2 Timothy 4:7 after you completed something?
2. What are areas that you normally make excuses in?
3. What is something you are determined to do and how do you know it?

Ephesians 4:32 (ESV)
Be kind to one another, tenderhearted, forgiving
one another, as God in Christ forgave you.

KINDNESS

the quality of being friendly, generous, and
considerate

Kindness can be better described as the
act of being kind just because it's the right thing
to do. If you do something good for the wrong
reasons, that is not a very kind thing to do. So
kindness encompasses the act and the motive.

One of the greatest commandments
from God is for us to love one another the same
way that we love ourselves. One of the ways to
show love for one another is to show kindness to
one another. When we talk about the grace and
mercy of God, we are referring to the kindness
that he continuously shows His people.

Kindness is the fuel for love. Kindness
benefits the person who is being kind, the
person who receives the kind act, and anybody
who sees the kindness. If people were kind,
there would be less crime and violence. If
people would show kindness to others, it would
help make the world a better place. And
sometimes, showing kindness can be as simple
as saying "thank you" or holding a door open for
someone.

Small acts of kindness can have huge
benefits to many people. We should be trying to

show kindness to as many people as we can. Think about how many people you might encounter in just one day. How many of these people do you do a kind act for? Challenge yourself to be kind to as many people as you can. Challenge yourself to make an effort to be kind.

Scripture to Remember

Proverbs 11:17 A man who is kind benefits himself, but a cruel man hurts himself. (ESV)

Questions for Growth

1. How does it make you feel when you see someone being kind?
2. How can being kind to other people be beneficial to you?
3. How could kindness make the community a better place?

Proverbs 13:4 (ESV)
*The soul of the sluggard craves and gets
nothing, while the soul of the diligent is richly
supplied.*

DILIGENCE

constantly working hard and carefully to
complete a task.

A diligent person not only works hard,
but they work smart and carefully as well. A
diligent person has a great work ethic and they
are very focused with what they are doing

King Solomon was assigned the task to
construct the Lord's Temple. It took him twenty
years to finally complete the assignment. He
was responsible for gathering all the workers,
equipment, and even establishing relationships
with other kingdoms to help him out. When he
finally completed the construction, God was very
pleased with what he had built. But King
Solomon had to constantly work hard and be
focused to have the temple completed. King
Solomon showed outstanding diligence as he
completed the temple.

We must be able to work diligently to
complete our tasks and assignments or to
accomplish any goal that we have set for
ourselves. When something becomes hard to
complete, it is our diligence, or our ability to work
hard and work smart and work carefully that will
help us to complete our tasks. If we only worked

hard but not with focus, we might spend time working hard at the wrong things. It takes a combination of work ethic and focus for us to complete anything that we want to complete. Without diligence, it becomes hard to become successful because lazy people do not accomplish things.

Diligence is working hard and working smart continuously. It takes persistence and focus on what we are trying to do. Think about any goals that you set or tasks that you have to complete. Do you work hard and focus on what you are supposed to be doing? Challenge yourself to approach anything that you have to do with diligence.

Scripture to Remember

Proverbs 10:4 A slack hand causes poverty, but the hand of the diligent makes rich. (ESV)

Questions for Growth

1. Why does laziness lead to poverty?
2. How does being diligent save time?
3. What is something great that someone has done without diligence?

Matthew 7:12 (NIV)
*So in everything, do to others what you would
have them do to you, for this sums up the Law
and the Prophets.*

RESPECT

a feeling of deep admiration for someone or
something because of what they did, can do, or
have accomplished

To show respect to someone is to value
them. Everybody has value, whether you see it
or not. When you value something or someone,
you take care of it and treat it or them kindly.
When you show respect to people or things, you
are valuing them and treating them kindly.

One of the major themes all throughout
the Bible is loving one another. We are to love
our neighbors as we love ourselves. You cannot
love a person if you do not respect a person.
The Bible teaches us to be kind to one another.
You cannot be kind to a person without showing
them some type of respect. Respect is the
foundation for all relationships and interactions
with people.

Respect goes a long way. It shapes how
people treat you and what they think about you
or what they would be willing to do for you.
When you do not show people respect, it causes
anger and fighting and they are less likely to
help you out or be kind to you. When you show
people respect, they in turn will do good things

for you. Or when someone shows you respect, you should do good things for them. We should also respect laws and rules and this means obeying them. Without respect, you will be unable to maintain relationships or get farther in life because no one will want to help you or be kind to you.

Respect is when you value something or someone so much, that you treat it or them in the right way. It is important that we always show respect first. Think about any situation that did not go well. Was there any lack of respect for that person or some rules? Challenge yourself to show respect to all people (which means valuing all people) and show respect to rules by following them.

Scripture to Remember

Romans 13:7 Pay to all what is owed to them: taxes to whom taxes are owed, revenue to whom revenue is owed, respect to whom respect is owed, honor to whom honor is owed (ESV)

Questions for Growth

1. What happens when we don't show the proper amount of respect?
2. How is disobedience similar to not showing respect?
3. What can you do to increase the amount of respect that you show people?

Proverbs 13:16 (ESV)
In everything the prudent acts with knowledge,
but a fool flaunts his folly.

PRUDENCE

acting with or showing care and thought for the future.

A prudent person is someone who uses wisdom, has good judgment, and makes wise decisions. They may not be the smartest person in the room, but they think before they speak and act. They not only think about the consequences of their actions, but they also make the decision that will have the best outcome.

Jesus is the perfect example of a prudent person. He lived the perfect life because he never sinned but on many occasions, he was put in tough situations where the wrong decision could've caused him to sin or even caused him to lose his life sooner than he had to. Jesus made his decisions thinking about the future and out of obedience to God.

We have to make decisions on a regular basis, some easy and some hard. Every decision that we make will have a consequence that follows it. If we are prudent we will make the right decision and ultimately it will have a positive impact on our lives and the lives of the people connected to us. Prudence leads to success while bad decision making leads to failure.

A prudent person is a person who makes wise decisions. They think and plan out carefully what they are about to do next. Think about how many decisions that you have to make on a daily basis. Based on what happens next, how often do you make wise choices? Challenge yourself to think about what the best possible thing to do is before you speak or act.

Scripture to Remember

Proverbs 14:15 The simple believe anything, but the prudent give thought to their steps. (NIV)

Questions for Growth

1. How can thinking about things instead of believing any and everything help you in life?
2. Why is important to read? (Think about what reading has to do with knowledge.)
3. Did you know that if you lack wisdom, you should ask God, who gives generously to all without finding fault, and it will be given to you?

Acts 8: 30-31 (NIV)
Then Philip ran up to the chariot and heard the man reading Isaiah the prophet. "Do you understand what you are reading?" Philip asked. "How can I," he said, "unless someone explains it to me?" So he invited Philip to come up and sit with him.

TEACHABLE

the ability to learn by being taught

Teachable means just what the word says, the ability to be taught. This means that we have to be humble and receptive to the information that someone wants to give us. Being teachable applies when we are being taught by another person.

There was an Ethiopian man reading the Bible and realized that he could not understand what he was reading. When asked if he understood what was going on, he said he could not understand unless someone taught him. From that moment, the Ethiopian man was able to learn something that he previously did not know. The Ethiopian man showed how teachable he was and was able to learn something new.

No one is born knowing everything and no one who is alive knows everything. Many times we may think we know something, but we could be completely wrong. We have to be teachable so that people can teach us the things that we need to know. We cannot always pick and choose who is going to teach us what we need to know, we just have to be able to learn it and that depends greatly on how humble we are and what our attitudes are like. If we are not teachable, people won't teach us what we need to know, and then we will not know the things that we need to know.

Teachable is the ability to be taught by someone else. It requires us to be humble and not act like we know everything already. Think about anybody who has tried to teach you something. Have they ever said that you are too proud or un-teachable or un-coachable? How did they treat you after this? Challenge yourself to be humble and learn as many things that you can from other people.

Scripture to Remember

Proverbs 13:18 Poverty and shame will come to him who disdains correction, But he who regards a rebuke will be honored. (NKJV)

Questions for Growth

1. How is being corrected similar to being taught?
2. Why is correction important in our lives?
3. Why does pride make it hard to be taught?

Matthew 14: 17-18 (NIV)
*"We have here only five loaves of bread and
two fish," they answered. "Bring them here to
me," he said."*

RESOURCEFULNESS

the ability to find solutions to problems using
what is available

A resourceful person is someone who
can take what they have and make it work. It is
when you encounter a problem and solve it
using whatever you currently have, even if it
doesn't seem like enough.

In the biblical days, there was not as
much technology and resources available as
there is now, but they still were able to do great
things. Enormous buildings were constructed,
great distances were traveled, and larger armies
were defeated by smaller armies. All of these
great things were accomplished because they
used what they had available. Jesus gives us an
excellent picture of this when he feeds the 5000
men with five loaves and two fish. They were
hungry but there was not enough food to feed
them all... or so they thought. Jesus took what
He had and made it work.

To accomplish any task or goal,
something has to be used. Often times it may
seem like we don't have the things that we need
to do what we need to do. We may even be in
situations where we can't afford to get what we

need. It is times like this when we must be resourceful. We have to take whatever it is that we already have, and make it work for us.

Resourcefulness is when you can take what you have and make it work. It is when you fully use your resources that you have available to you whether those resources may be big or small. Think about what you have and what you need to accomplish. Do you see that you don't have enough or are you looking for a way to make it work? Challenge yourself to use the tools and resources that you have when you don't think that you have enough.

Scripture to Remember

Proverbs 30:26 The conies are but a feeble folk, yet they make their houses in the rocks (KJV)

Questions for Growth

1. What resources and tools do you have available to you?
2. Why do we have to be able to make the most out of what we already have?
3. How can being resourceful save time, energy, and stress?

Genesis 2:18 (ESV)
…It is not good that the man should be alone; I
will make him a helper fit for him.

TEAMWORK

the process of working collaboratively with a
group of people in order to achieve a goal.

Teamwork means that a group of people
will work together with one another to achieve
the same goal. Teamwork means that I am
looking out for the best interest of the group, not
myself.

Since the very beginning, God decided
that it is not good for Man to be alone and that
everyone needs a helper. We wouldn't need a
helper if we could do everything on our own.
This requires us to be able to work together with
another person. Even God utilizes teamwork.
The Holy Trinity consist of three beings, God the
Father, Jesus, and the Holy Spirit. These three
beings are three completely different beings all
working together; they are using perfect
teamwork to carry out the Will of God.

Many times in life we will be forced to
work in a team. Whether it is on an athletic
team, completing a school project, or completing
a task at work; at some point we will all have to
work on a team with other people. If we are
unable to utilize good teamwork, how can we
accomplish things? In fact, it is easier to
accomplish a task when I am working with a

team instead of trying to do it by myself. We all need each other and we all need to know how to work together. The most important thing about teamwork is that when we are on a team, we need to carry our weight and do the part that is assigned to us to the very best of our ability.

On a team, if one person fails, then everyone fails. If one person succeeds then everyone succeeds. There is no 'I' in team. It's about working together for the good of the group, not the good of yourself. Think about how many different teams or groups you may be a part of. Are you doing all you can for the team to achieve the team's goal? Challenge yourself to do your part to the best of your ability whenever you are working in a team.

Scripture to Remember

Genesis 11:6 And the Lord said, "Behold, they are one people, and they have all one language, and this is only the beginning of what they will do. And nothing that they propose to do will now be impossible for them." (ESV)

Questions for Growth

1. What do you think Genesis 11:6 means?
2. Why is it important for you to be able to work in a team?
3. How can working as a team make things better?

Joshua 1:9 (ESV)
*Have I not commanded you? Be strong and
courageous. Do not be frightened, and do not be
dismayed, for the Lord your God is with you
wherever you go."*

COURAGE

a willingness to do something that frightens you

Courage is when you are afraid to do
something, but you do it anyway. Courage is
facing your fears. When you know something is
hard or difficult and you normally would be too
fearful to do it, it is courage that allows you to do
it anyway.

For many years, Joshua spent his time
serving as the assistant to Moses. He simply did
what Moses would command him to do. One
day, Moses died and someone had to take his
spot. Joshua went from serving one man to
leading thousands of people and he was afraid,
very afraid. But God commanded him to be
courageous in what he was about to do. Joshua
went on to be a great leader of the people of
Israel as he conquered other kings and served
God.

We all need courage to excel in life. As
we try to reach our goals, there will always be
something that comes up that we are afraid of;
things that if we conquer it, we will continue on
but if we are afraid and never do it, it could stop
us reaching our goals. When people don't have

courage, they choose to not do some of the things that they need to do simply because they are scared. If we go through life not doing things simply because we are scared of them, we will never get to the place that we want to be.

Courage is continuing on even in the face of fear; or sometimes danger. We have to have courage to help us persevere through the times when we are afraid to try something new. Think about anytime that you have been afraid to do something. Do your fears take control and stop you, or do you have the courage to continue on? Challenge yourself to face your fears and be courageous when you are afraid.

Scripture to Remember

2 Timothy 1:7 For God hath not given us the spirit of fear; but of power, and of love, and of a sound mind. (KJV)

Questions for Growth

1. How can power, love, and a sound mind help you be more courageous?
2. Why is it important to face our fears?
3. Have you ever faced one of your fears before? How did you feel afterwards?

Matthew 9:36 (ESV)
When he saw the crowds, he had compassion
for them, because they were harassed and
helpless, like sheep without a shepherd.

COMPASSION

sympathetic pity and concern for the sufferings
or misfortunes of others

Compassion literally means to suffer
together. It is that feeling that arises when you
notice someone who is less fortunate than
yourself, and you feel compelled to help them
out

All throughout the life of Jesus, he
constantly shows compassion on all the people
whom he would meet. Jesus was 100% God
and 100% Man, so He was greater than any
person who he would come into contact with.
Whenever he noticed that he met a person who
was sick, or lost, or mistreated, he did not turn
his nose up at them or make them feel bad for
being in a bad spot or pick on them for being
less fortunate than himself, He would choose to
do all He could to help them out.

All throughout life we are going to come
in contact with a variety of people who have a
variety of different situations. Some of these
people will be more fortunate than ourselves and
some of these people will be less fortunate than
ourselves. When we meet someone in a less
fortunate situation than ourselves, it is important
that we treat them kindly and offer to help them
out. You never know what could happen in your
life and one day you are going to be in a bad

situation and need the help of someone who is more fortunate than you are. It would be a shame for someone that could help you to leave you in a bad situation just because they thought they were better than you. If we are going to really love all the people around us, we have to know how to treat people who are less fortunate than ourselves and we use compassion for this.

Compassion is another level of kindness. It is when we notice someone who needs help so we feel the need to help them out rather than pick on them or ignore them. Think of the people you come in contact with and think of how much compassion you show for them. Are you the type of person that would give spare change to homeless person or pick on them because they might smell? Challenge yourself to go through your day trying to show compassion to people who are less fortunate than you are.

Scripture to Remember

1 Peter 3:8 Finally, all of you, be like minded, be sympathetic, love one another, be compassionate and humble (NIV)

Questions for Growth

1. Why is compassion important?
2. What is one way that showing compassion can improve the community?
3. How does it make you feel when you do something good for someone else?

Psalm 30:5 (NKJV)
*...Weeping may endure for a night. But joy
comes in the morning.*

RESILIENCE

the ability to recover from difficulties;

Resilience is the "bounce back" effect—
to get knocked down and get back up. A resilient
person can take a lick'n and keep on tick'n.

All the people who ever served God
faithfully and completed a task had to be
resilient. Often times they would come against
opposition that sometimes beat them. When the
apostles would go out to preach, often times
they would be unwelcomed and sometimes even
attacked. But they believed in what they were
doing and kept going. When they would get
knocked down or treated unfairly, they didn't
mope around or feel sorry for themselves. They
didn't let their painful circumstances stop them.
They got back up and continued with what they
had to do.

Life is tough. Life knocks you down. No
matter what you're doing or how careful you try
to be or how good you try to be, you will get
knocked down at some point. The question is,
what will you do next? You have to be resilient;
you have to be able to dust yourself off and keep
on going. If every time you get knocked down
you quit, you will never accomplish anything and

you will never be successful. Whenever you fall down, you get back up.

Resilience is when you can get back up after being knocked down; when you can continue on in the face of adversity. Think about anytime in your life when things didn't go the way you expected. Did you let that stop you or did you find a way to keep on going? Challenge yourself to keep on going after you get knocked down.

Scripture to Remember

Proverbs 24:16 For a righteous man falls seven times, and rises again... (NASB)

Questions for Growth

1. Why do you need to be a resilient person?
2. What should you do when you fall or fail at something?
3. What is one area in your life you can show more resilience in?

Matthew 6:14-15 (ESV)
*For if you forgive others their trespasses, your
heavenly Father will also forgive you, but if you
do not forgive others their trespasses, neither
will your Father forgive your trespasses..*

FORGIVENESS

to stop feeling anger toward something or
someone who has done something wrong and to
stop blaming them

Forgiveness is when someone does
something wrong to you and you no longer treat
them like they did something wrong to you.

One of the major themes in the Bible is
forgiveness. The greatest act of love was when
Jesus went to the cross for us. But, He did it so
that we can be forgiven; so that we would not be
punished for the sin in our lives. Jesus even
begged that forgiveness be shown to the very
people who were stoning and hurting Him.
Because we all are sinful, we all need to be
forgiven. God says, that He will forgive you to
the same capacity that you forgive others.

Forgiveness is something that if we
learn how to do, it will make our lives much
better. The purpose of forgiveness is to make
you feel better, not the other person. No matter
what, somebody will do something that offends
you or makes you upset. If you never forgive
them, you will always walk around being upset
or angry with that person. Forgiveness allows

you to let go of that negative feeling; it will help
you feel better, which will help your attitude,
which will help your behavior, which effects the
outcome of your life. We have to forgive to live.

Forgiveness is a very loving and kind
act to do but it benefits you more than anything.
It allows you to let go of the negative emotions
down in your heart. It is also how we have God
show forgiveness to us. If we don't show
forgiveness to people, how can we expect God
to forgive us? Think about anybody who has
upset you lately. Have you forgiven them?
Challenge yourself to model your forgiveness
after Jesus's forgiveness.

Scripture to Remember

Matthew 6:12 And forgive us our debts, as we
also have forgiven our debtors. (ESV)

Questions for Growth

1. What does Mathew 6:12 mean?
2. Why is forgiveness a necessary part of
    life?
3. How can forgiveness make you feel
    better? If forgiveness doesn't make you
    feel better, why is that?

<u>Chronological Order</u>

Goal Setting	Day 1	Sacrifice	Day 17
Character	Day 2	Perseverance	Day 18
Influence	Day 3	Humility	Day 19
Attitude	Day 4	Determination	Day 20
Role-Model	Day 5	Kindness	Day 21
Honesty	Day 6	Diligent	Day 22
Decision Making	Day 7	Respect	Day 23
Integrity	Day 8	Prudence	Day 24
Consequences	Day 9	Teachable	Day 25
Responsibility	Day 10	Resourcefulness	Day 26
Self - Control	Day 11	Teamwork	Day 27
Accountability	Day 12	Courage	Day 28
Discipline	Day 13	Compassion	Day 29
Work Ethic	Day 14	Resilience	Day 30
Relational	Day 15	Forgiveness	Day 31
Excellence	Day 16		

Alphabetical Order

Accountability	Day 12	Integrity	Day 8
Attitude	Day 4	Kindness	Day 21
Character	Day 2	Perseverance	Day 18
Compassion	Day 29	Prudence	Day 24
Consequences	Day 9	Relational	Day 15
Courage	Day 28	Resilience	Day 30
Decision Making	Day 7	Resourcefulness	Day 26
Determination	Day 20	Respect	Day 23
Diligent	Day 22	Responsibility	Day 10
Discipline	Day 13	Role-Model	Day 5
Excellence	Day 16	Sacrifice	Day 17
Forgiveness	Day 31	Self - Control	Day 11
Goal Setting	Day 1	Teachable	Day 25
Honesty	Day 6	Teamwork	Day 27
Humility	Day 19	Work Ethic	Day 14
Influence	Day 3		

Success Under Construction

Success Under Construction